I CHOSE TO
Wait

Joi Vaughn

ISBN 978-1-64468-749-9 (Paperback)
ISBN 978-1-64468-750-5 (Digital)

Copyright © 2020 Joi Vaughn
All rights reserved
First Edition

All rights reserved. No part of this publication may be reproduced, distributed, or transmitted in any form or by any means, including photocopying, recording, or other electronic or mechanical methods without the prior written permission of the publisher. For permission requests, solicit the publisher via the address below.

Covenant Books, Inc.
11661 Hwy 707
Murrells Inlet, SC 29576
www.covenantbooks.com

It was August of 2006, I was eight and a half months pregnant with our fourth child when I discovered that my husband was having an affair. I had noticed that his attitude and behavior were different. He started listening to strange music and the way that he spoke to me was strange and different. He started staying out late without rhyme or reason. He started lying more concerning his whereabouts and his stories were inconsistent. His cell phone was always hidden and password-protected. Another key indicator that things had changed was the way he spoke to me. I knew he was being influenced by someone else because I knew him. I knew the way he talked and the kind of music he listened to. His priorities had changed as well as his demeanor. The mistress may not always be a person but a thing, an addiction, a habit, or hobby. As long as it's causing his/her attention and affection for you to be divided and/or taken away, there is still a problem that must be dealt with. Whatever or whoever the mistress is, please keep reading.

With much persistence and curiosity, I had gained access to his cell phone. What I discovered was several dozen text messages between him and another woman. I believe I heard a voice mail too. When I confronted him with the evidence, he could no longer lie or deny the truth. He finally admitted that yes, he was having an affair. We tried to "work" on it but that false effort ended up being him playing with my emotions. He had no intention of working out our issues. We tried to talk about it but she had her grip on him. Like the Bible says in Proverbs 5:3-5, "For the lips of a strange woman drop as a honeycomb, and her mouth is smoother than oil, But her end is bitter as wormwood, sharp as a two-edged sword, her feet go down to death; and her steps take hold on hell."

It was absolutely amazing (not in a good way) that I saw Scripture play out right in front of my eyes like a movie or a reality TV show. The things that my husband went through, which I talk about through this book, directly coincide with Scripture. The warnings, the judgment came to pass in his life. God practically stripped everything from him but his life and his income. This woman had taken ahold of his mind; she took over his thoughts and controlled his behavior and attitude. It was almost like he had been alien-abducted and they gave me this fake duplicate. I only recognized his face, nothing else about him was familiar. He became a stranger to me, and by this point, we had been married for seven years. He met her on his lunch break, at a KFC, and she approached him. The strange thing was, I had fantasized about the woman that my husband would cheat on me with; and lo and behold, this woman looked identical to the woman I imagined. As a man thinketh—so is he. I had created my enemy.

Getting back to the moment of the confrontation, I was absolutely devastated. Not only did I have to deal with the stress of finding this out, I was still very much pregnant. I'd been having Braxton-Hicks for a few months before that. Things had been shaky between us for the past several months because I was pregnant. He did not want a fourth child! I remember the night I got pregnant. We had just bought a brand-new house and we made love and did not use protection. From that moment, he resented me for it. We had three children already and had been struggling to make ends meet. I knew he did not want a fourth child.

I'm not saying that was the reason why he cheated but I knew the marriage was shaky. For example, we had a birthday party for one of our sons and we were at a park in our neighborhood. It was just the two of us the party and all we did was curse and yell at each other for a good thirty minutes. There was something about that moment that I will never forget. I wasn't listening to his needs and he wasn't listening to mine. One thing about being in any relationship—you never know what the other is thinking and you never quite know when the other person is on the brink of leaving or having an affair. No one always expresses all their thoughts and feelings to you.

I gave birth to our son two or three weeks after I found out about the affair. When I was in the hospital giving birth, my husband was on the phone with his mistress. He kept leaving the room, she kept calling and texting. He was fully distracted. The emotional toll was enough to send me clean off the edge. Life, at that moment, was completely unbearable. God had given me more than I could handle and the way of escape wouldn't be revealed for more than a year later. The birth of our youngest took a toll on my body to the point where the doctor strongly advised not having any more. But four is enough. My husband was not attentive because he was juggling two women. Men are not multitask-oriented. They will never be successful at adultery.

While driving me home from the hospital, sitting in the back seat of the car with our newborn son, he told me that I needed to leave. I hadn't even made it home yet. Within a few days, I was on the road with a newborn and my third youngest child. I would spend my entire maternity leave at my grandmother's house out of state. My friend threw me a baby shower a few weeks after I had arrived. He drove down for that and, mind you, I hadn't seen her yet. I hadn't seen the mistress. The only image of her was what I pictured she would look like in my mind. Suddenly he was talking like he was open to us working things out. I didn't believe him; he was too undecided and indecisive. His words were too weak; I felt no stability in what he said.

While at the shower, I was, of course, watching him like a hawk. He had never really paid attention to my best friend before, at least, not that I had noticed. There was a moment when I looked at him and he was looking up at her. She was standing up at the time and was also tall. From the look on his face, I knew the woman he was cheating on me with was tall; it was just something about the way he looked at her. I knew the presence of God and my discernment was in full force during this time. God has always walked with me but it was during this time that I knew that He was carrying me while we walked. My dream life has been very vivid since I was a kid. God used my dreams, He gave me visions, He was all over me—all around me.

At that moment, when I really paid attention to the look on my husband's face when he was looking at my friend, I felt that was God letting me know that he was still in a relationship with her. He stayed the weekend and drove back to our home. I cried when he left. After he returned home, it was like the conversations we had about restoring the marriage never took place. He was very temperamental with me, and it seemed like he was falling in love with the adulteress.

There were several very positive things that developed during this time away from him and while at Grandma's house. I got closer to my aunt. Let's call her Angela, and she really helped me see how having an effective relationship with the Lord and a consistent prayer life would be a great asset in my life. Angela would then introduce me to a woman I now consider my spiritual mom. Not only is she a prophet but is also a psychologist. Who wouldn't need to have someone with biblical knowledge, prophetic, and has a psychology background during a time like this? She was like pure gold to me, a real live gift from God. Let's call her Gloria. I got the best of both worlds, all in one person. I was able to counsel with her every week. She helped me deal with what I was going through in my marriage and helped me to bond and depend on God. She reestablished my need to know and have a relationship with God on my own and not through someone else. I am thankful, to this day, that I had my aunt and Gloria's support.

If you are going through a situation like this, it will be more difficult to get through it without God. There is no escaping His presence, the need for Him in your life. There is no escaping your need for His hand, and there is no escaping your need for His guidance. If you try to go at this alone, you will make bad choices. For example, the likelihood that you'll end up in bed with somebody else is more probable than you could even imagine. By doing this, you could potentially end up divorcing prematurely. You end up exposing your children to people that they don't need to be exposed to because you acted emotionally and didn't think things though. It is amazing how irrational our decisions are when we are going through an emotional trauma. That's why people end up marrying the mistress and then end up divorced again. People in affairs don't talk about the future or their fears. They don't talk about how the children could be impacted for the rest of their lives. Why would they start to think of others? Why would they think of the people they are hurting? That would take the fun out of the affair. God will help you stabilize your mind, attitude, thoughts, actions, and behavior. Allow God to come in and help navigate you through this as well as day-to-day life.

One of the first things I remember my spiritual mom said to me was, she was not going to be God for me she would help me build a relationship with Him, teach me how to pray, but I would have to forge my own relationship with God.

Sharing the Details of the State of Your Marriage

Sharing is caring right? Not always. You have to be mindful of who you share those play-by-play situations with. There were only a few members of my family that knew the intimate details of what was going on in my marriage. I believed that God would restore my marriage and I didn't want all of my husband's dirt out in the streets. I also didn't want folks who didn't share my belief in the power of God to dissuade me in my journey. I'm glad I made the decision to protect my spouse because he had built rapport with my family. They had all adopted him and I didn't want to tarnish or ruin the relationships that he had with them. I chose to think things through and not just look for someone to take pity on me and judge him. What I mean by that is, let's take my aunt for example. Although I loved her dearly and she was like a second mother to me, I enjoyed talking to her and spending time at her home. I knew she loved me. However, she did not have a relationship with the Lord and had been in a twenty-year relationship with a man that she wasn't not married to. What strong marital advice could I get from her? Why would I tell my best friend or confide in her so much that I'm taking everything she says and running with it when she was an unmarried female?

I used wisdom when it came to who I would expose all the dirt. I chose someone who I felt was safe, wouldn't always take my side but showed great care and compassion for what I was going through. Someone who had been married longer than I was, with children, and married young. Someone who had a mature relationship with God and could hear Him speak. Their relationship with God was not fake or phony. It was real! No one other than God knows the truth of what my life was like between 2006 and the end of 2007.

Before you share information about your marriage, take time to investigate the lifestyle of that person. Look at the way they live their lives and use that to help you judge whether or not they are trustworthy enough to know what's going on in your life. Are they truly able to advise you? Only talk to those who can give you sound godly advice. You cannot think that your unsaved friend whose only ever been labeled a "girlfriend" or "side chick" can give you sound marital advice. Don't think that your mom who has never been married but has multiple experiences with live-in boyfriends could possibly give good direction. It's not going to happen. Even those who have been married and it ended in divorce may still hold bitterness toward marriage. They may not be as bias as you would need them to be. If you don't have anybody in your immediate circle, then you should be able to find a godly woman in your local church who represents the Lord and can give you the right advice. Ultimately the decision is yours to make. You do have the option to dissolve the marriage. Although it is not God's initial design or first response, He does give us that allowance to leave the marriage when a spouse deserts the relationship.

This book will be about what I went through, but it will also be about my journey with God. My relationship with the Lord didn't truly begin until I hit rock bottom. Before all this happened, I rarely prayed and barely read my Bible. We would go to church but it was like going to work. It was like a check mark on a weekly to-do list. But pain will open your eyes and make you run to the one who can heal your hurt. That's when I truly saw who God was in my life. I had to need Him and see Him as my Father. Not just the Father or a friend I would call on an as needed basis. He was also a mother, friend, counselor, doctor, and a lawyer. He was all-encompassing. He was love and support. Compassion and grace. He would take no time to correct me when I was wrong. Now I am going to step away from discussing the affair for just a bit, and travel back to my childhood. I feel the need to dive into why, I believe past hurts play a part in why we do what we do.

I lived with my grandparents then grandparent until adulthood. My mother was there for the first several years of my life, but then drug abuse took her away from me. What is left for a little girl with no mother or father? My father was young and totally irresponsible. He did his own thing all of my life. He was always in and out, absolutely no consistency from him whatsoever. I was basically an orphan. My grandfather was not a blood relative. He married my grandmother after she had my mother. My grandmother's husband was a pedophile. With no parents to protect me, I was sexually assaulted from a very young age until about nine or ten.

What I went through as a child, I believe, played a role in why my husband cheated on me. The reason I say this is because for many years, early on, in our marriage, I had undeniably no appetite for sex. We were intimate before marriage and had no problem with sex whatsoever. We were having sex all the time, but something happened the day I said I do to my husband. The desire to have sex was no longer available to me. No matter how much I cried or how much I prayed or begged God, it did not come back. A part of me felt like the enemy created another weapon against me as a result of me being molested. This weapon would cause conflict in my marriage. When you marry, you're making a covenant not only with your husband but to God. You're picking a side before and choosing to live by God's design.

Before marriage, I was choosing to live worldly. I was operating outside of the will of God which means in the flesh. Your flesh is on fire and doing whatever feels good. But once I made a covenant with God and with my husband, I had chosen a different side. A man wants sex; a married man should expect it. A young married man, wants, expects, and needs it to help build a bond with his wife. That was one dagger causing constant arguments for years. Besides being frigid for years, I had a very strong distrust in my husband. I completely struggled trusting men and trusting in men. My dad was not a real part of my life, being molested by my grandfather, and having boyfriends cheat and lie—all of that played a role in my marriage.

We don't realize how much baggage and weight we carry into our marriages. If we never take the time to go to counseling and or go through deliverance and get healed from our past, the things that we went through as children or as or teenagers will sit and fester and manifest in ways we never imagined. With some of us having been molested, raped, abused emotionally and physically or having been abandoned, we then create a different suitcase packed with those traumas and memories. We just stack them up and keep carrying them with us through every relationship, collecting more and more baggage as we go and hoarding it all. Instead of going into the relationship ready to build from the ground up, we end up going into with a house full because we never unpacked. We never exposed it, we never talked about it, never got help, and never grieved it. All that pain creates a whole house full of junk.

Growing up, I knew how to keep secrets but was never taught the necessity of getting help or knowing when you need help, knowing when something you've gone through shouldn't be kept secret. We don't push anyone to talk and we really didn't advise anyone to go to therapy. My family didn't know anything about going through healing and deliverance at church. We were taught you'll get over it, just don't talk about it and it'll go away. For many years, I had buried the molestation so deep that it was almost like it never happened. I had learned to mask it.

I had a cousin that lived around the corner from me while I was growing up. She lived with her grandmother too. Her mother and father weren't married; they were young in running the streets. She was raped by one of her uncles. Child Services got involved and my cousin ended up in foster care. At a very young age, I knew that she wasn't in a home with anyone who knew or loved her. I knew her life was hard and I was about ten or twelve years old making these assessments. No one said to me, "If you tell anyone about what happened, you'll end up like your cousin." Her life traumas kept mine silent. From then on, it stayed buried. It wasn't until maybe five to six years after we reconciled that I started dealing with some very severe depression and ended up in therapy. It stemmed from never dealing with the sexual abuse. So here it is, about thirty years later and that trauma is still there. It could no longer be kept a secret.

It was October of 2006, and my maternity leave was coming to an end. I was stressed out over going back. Not knowing what's happening in my home. Not knowing if my husband was going to let me in the house or if I was going to have to quit my job and move back in with my grandmother with four kids. My husband decided to let his brother, who was married with a kid, move into our home. They were heavy marijuana and cigarette smokers. My mother-in-law had never attempted to visit our home other than when I left and came to LA. That little fact should provide some insight into that part of my life. I was already dealing with enough on my plate and had no intention of sharing a home with them. That would have added to the chaos that was already in motion. Angela and Gloria knew that I was leaving and driving back home. I didn't know they were on the phone, praying for me.

When I pulled up at my house, the front door was open and my husband's car was on the street. Something was going on but I didn't know what. I walked in to see that my husband was actively packing up my brother-in-law and his wife to take them back home, which was five hours away, the same day that I got home. By the grace of God, I did not have to spend one night in my house with them in it; they were gone. The only thing I had to contend with was the smell of smoke that seemed to be ingrained in the walls and carpet. I had a hard time adjusting to being back with everything that had happened so far. I also believed that his mistress was a regular visitor in my home and possibly slept in my bed. Just nasty as hell, disgusting, hood rat heffa (excuse me, but I had to go all the way off real quick).

Now that I was back home, had returned to work, and gained some normality in my life, I began to have weekly therapy sessions over the phone with Gloria. I told her that I felt things had happened in my home, things that were vile and dirty. Things that were disrespectful to me and my marriage. I didn't feel peace. She said I had to take authority over it and so she told me what to say when I prayed. It took some time but, eventually, I felt like it was my home again. After his quick trip to drop his brother and wife back to their residence, he came back to our home. We tried to share the same home but we had been arguing constantly. All that drama wasn't healthy for us or our children. The hoe-stress made sure he had hickeys on his neck and he was consistently lying about his whereabouts. Telling me that he was working extra hours when he was really with her. I no longer knew him and stopped having sex with him.

Sex is not going to save your marriage; it's not going to keep a man. It will only quench his thirst *temporarily*. The sooner you learn that fact, the better off you will be. Remember, all women have vaginas—there isn't one made of gold. We all have the same body parts. If he has not made the decision to commit, he will not. I had to stop using my body to try to win him over; I had to use the instructions and tools God was giving me.

January 2007, I was done having a fake marriage and uncommitted husband. I was done with being talked down to. He spoke to me without a filter; he was so nasty to me, all we did was argue. I had thought about this decision for months, and it was one night that I said, "You need to leave!" I remember I was so angry; my whole body was on fire. My blood pressure was though the roof. I hit him and he hit me back; he pushed me up against the wall and I remember I hit my tailbone real hard. That wasn't my husband, my sweetheart, my baby daddy. It was like somebody else was controlling his mind. It was like his was a total stranger, like we married at first sight. He moved out and went to live with two of his male coworkers. He moved thirty minutes from us.

My husband was always a very active father to our kids. Always around them, spending time with them, building individual relationships with them, talking to them, and teaching them things. But he began having an affair, all that stopped. The kids suffered, they didn't know or understand why Dad wasn't there after school or when they went to bed. They didn't understand why he wasn't there on the weekends. Why he was, all of sudden, so distant. He just wasn't the same person anymore.

I don't think it had been two months before that living arrangement came to an immediate end. Two of them got into a physical altercation and ended up getting into trouble with the police. My husband had never been in trouble with the law before and his life was turned upside down that quickly. The whole time that we were separated, life became very uneasy for him. His car was repossessed, he had to go to court over the issue with his roommates, he moved several times. He lost a lot of weight and was already on the thin side. He started smoking marijuana, he was drinking and anxious—just a total transformation from who he was. He almost lost his job because he suffered from insomnia and had overslept several times. He had no car and relied on public transportation which is really a last resort where we live.

Fight or Flight

With everything going on between us and how he treated me meant it was time for me to make a decision. Was I going to stay in and fight for our marriage and family or walk away? I also had to choose to begin a prayer life and be consistent in it. Which meant I had to go to church, spend time in God's Word, and study. Ask the Lord what I needed to do and what He wanted from me. I had to be focused and intentional with my finances as well. I no longer had the flexibility of having a second income. Now I was raising four children, paying a mortgage, car payment, and day care expenses on one income. I remember that it was about a month after he left that I got promoted and a raise. It was the best thing that could have happened at that time because my husband had taken income from us. It was very difficult for me to maintain all of that on one income.

God is good; the Lord had blessed me to find a day care provider two doors down from the one who wouldn't help me out when she knew that my husband had left me. The new day care provider was $300 less a month and allowed me to pay her once a month. My household expenses ended up being 90 percent of my monthly income. The new position would present additional blessings from the Lord. He used men to pour into my bosom. I was walking in a Luke 2:52 season ("And Jesus increased in wisdom, and stature, and in favor with God and man").

My supervisor and my coworkers were very generous; they blessed me with gift cards for groceries, movie tickets, restaurants, and cash. I was able to work overtime to make more money. The Lord had strategically placed me in the pathways of people who would be a blessing to me during this time. I had started praying with my children and my middle son who has always been chunky.

He was nine pounds when he was born. When it was his turn to pray, he would always say, "Lord, we thank you for the food," among other things. But that was a common theme in his prayers. We ended up getting blessed with a $300-gift card from my boss; it was enough for a month's worth of groceries. God hears your prayers; He hears the prayers of children. He will not be manipulated by what we say when we pray. It is solely up to Him to respond and when to respond.

By now, we had been married for seven years, together for ten, and I was about twenty-nine years old. My whole adult life, I had only been with him. He got to a point where he didn't want to talk to me on the phone. Sometimes when I would call him, he had the audacity to respond back to me via text and say, "Let's talk via text." It was a very controlled method of communication. If I began to question him or if he felt I was nagging him too much, he would hang up the phone on me. He wouldn't answer when/if I tried calling back. If I started crying in the midst of a conversation, he would hang up on me. If started talking about the other woman or asking him when he was going to come back, he would start to yell or curse at me. It was a type of controlled style of communication, that allowed me to see that the man who I married and had four children with treated me with so little dignity or respect. It was no doubt an adjustment for me.

In the midst of all this was God. In the most difficult of times, He will call you to rise above it, to maintain a lifestyle of holiness and righteousness. There I was, crying daily, three to four times a day, having bouts of anxiety and depression, and God was dealing with me about forgiving this woman. Forgive her for attempting to do what she could to destroy our marriage and having sex with my husband. I can remember standing in my bedroom, calling her on the phone, and telling her I forgave her for having an affair with my husband. This was the same woman that sent me text messages to tell me what was going to happen with my house and that my husband was going to leave me. He was trying to get me to sell our home. She had all these plans and made all these decisions. I politely let her know she had no authority over me or my home. She had no authority over the decisions that needed to be made in my life.

One of the many things I regretted not doing, while we were separated, was filing for child support. I was silly and easily manipulated by him. Ladies, you must take whatever steps necessary to stabilize your lifestyle and the lifestyle of your children. I did not do my homework like I should have. I just let him take his income completely away and I ended up struggling to make ends meet while trying to raise four children. The cheapest items I could afford to feed them was bologna and cheese, bread and noodles, dollar-store cheap food in order to put food in their bellies. I had little money left in the bank once I paid my bills. Surviving on twenty dollars a week for lunch and going to Taco Bell, places where I could eat for ninety-nine cents. It got to a point where my son asked me when was I going to cook. How do you have the heart to tell a child you don't have the money to buy chicken and ground beef? All we could afford was what was in the refrigerator. It was a very difficult position for me, but when you're in a situation like that, know it's only for a season. It is not symbolic of the rest of your life.

The Decision

If you decide to endure the struggle and fight to save your marriage or to end it, you have the right to decide. It's not something you need to decide on right away. Give yourself time to really think about whether or not waiting for your spouse is worth the energy and effort you'll need to put into saving the marriage. Weigh your options and pray. Don't try to avoid finalizing if you should fight or quit. Waiting around will only make things worse. Commit to giving yourself the opportunity to grieve your current circumstances because the way you feel is equal to the feeling of losing a loved one. You do feel like something or someone died.

After some time has passed and the pain is not so severe and you can think clearly and without so much emotion, determine whether you want to stay or move on. You are not a failure if you decide to divorce. Not everyone can handle the pressures that come along with fighting. It does take a severe emotional, mental, and psychological toll on you. You almost feel like you are losing your mind at times. It takes strength, courage, endurance, and tenacity to stay in the ring when you can't see who all the opponents in your fight are. The Bible says, "For we wrestle not against flesh and blood, but against principalities, against powers, against the rulers of the darkness of this world, against spiritual wickedness in high places."

The Kiddos

If you should decide to stay, make sure your spouse is keeping up with raising and spending quality time with the children. Make sure you work through the process of getting child support and/or alimony payments. The financial responsibility of managing the children is not all on you. You did not create those children by yourself and you should not have to take care of them by yourself. If your partner falls short on ensuring the children are maintained, seek an attorney and take them to court. Try to keep them in fun activities during nonschool days/hours to help them deal with this transition. Keep open communication with them as I am sure they will have lots of questions. Do *not* tear down your spouse to them. Your feelings toward your partner should not be transferred to them. Do *not* contaminate the children against their mother or father.

I Chose to Stay and Fight

My thoughts became my beliefs, my beliefs became my actions, and my actions controlled my behavior. I struggled greatly with that decision. Anything he did or said made me believe we would end up divorced. When you have no control over what's going on in your life, you tend to go with what you see or hear. Staying in to fight was like being wedged between two concrete walls that were smashing the breath out of my body. I had anxiety attacks, I cried when I woke up in the morning, and cried myself to sleep some nights—especially in the beginning.

However, the Word of God says, "Trust in God with all your heart and lean not on your own understanding in all your ways submit to him and he will make your paths straight" (Proverbs 3:5). I had to learn how to keep my eyes focused on the Lord and trust in His promises. In spite of all that I was going through with my husband, God was still faithful. I felt His presence constantly, and He was always speaking to me verbally and through dreams and even visions. There were many times, throughout the months we were separated, where God gave me and my children favor. My kids were ten, eight, three, six months and they needed shoes. My youngest son had never had a pair of shoes. I kept hearing God tell me to take them shopping for shoes but I'm like, I don't have the kind of money to get them all a decent pair of sneakers. There was a Sears outlet store that I would see driving home from work every day.

I think it was a Friday or Saturday night and I got the kids together and took them over to Sears, hoping I could find shoes for at least the older two. I was not expecting to purchase three pairs of shoes and only spend forty-five dollars. When I needed laundry soap and had very little money, I went to Target and found a ninety-six-ounce bottle of laundry soap on clearance for six dollars. My cable was cut off, that was a total luxury for me and the kids at that time. I called the cable company, they turned my cable service back on for twenty dollars.

God wasn't only blessing me materially but stabilizing other areas of my life by filling voids and wounds left by my natural parents or people I once looked up to or admired. He means the world to me. Developing that belief, I would confidently recommend. He walked me back from the edge so many times. He is all-inclusive and is everything to me. Knowing that he is everything to me, I would truly and confidently recommend that if you don't know God. If you don't have a prayer life or if you've never prayed. It's only too late if you are no longer with the living. Having a relationship with the Lord will change your life for the good. He's not just going to focus on the broken marriage, He's going to focus on the broken individuals that are in the marriage. He has to remove, repair, introduce new things to the entities involved before He can bring them back together in order for the relationship to work. It would defeat His purpose if he left you both the same and then brought you back together. You would end up back in the same predicament you were in before you separated.

Although you are working on yourself, learning how to be independent and how to be single mother/father you, don't use your alone time to mope and moan. You must continue to grow and learn from your mistakes. You should also take this time to analyze your relationships with friends and family members. If the relationship is not strong or purposeful other than being a blood relative or having a long-standing history with that person, consider removing them from your inner circle and, possibly, your life. If you already have an idea of who to remove but lack the courage to end communication, pray about it and ask God to give you strength. This is not being mean or inconsiderate—it's growth.

As a plant grows, old leaves or deferment steams have to be pruned. You are going through a pruning process. You may still see those people; however, the access or privileged information you used to share with them will no longer be available. These unnecessary ankle weights in your life are just taking up space, reminding you of your past, and right now, you can't focus on the things of old. Moving forward, you have to be future-focused at all times. You may have grown up in a household where the Lord wasn't a priority or you only went to church on Easter and Mother's Day. With being future-focused, you're going to need Him more than just two days a year. You will need Him daily; you will need Him hour by hour, moment by moment to build up your strength. There are going to be times that things will happen that are just going to shut you down mentally and emotionally. If you don't know the sweet sound of the Holy Spirit's voice, encouraging you to fight, you will lose the battle.

Sucker Punched

One day, I had to pick up the kids from my husband's apartment. It was a Sunday; the enemy always throws dirty punches. I got over to his apartment, not knowing she was there. I don't think, up until that moment, that I had seen her up close or close enough to know who she was. My kids were in the car; I had to back my car out of the parking stall at the apartment complex. My middle son was sitting in the passenger seat, and he said, "Mom, that's her."

I had a sports car at the time and it would have taken three seconds to run her down with my car. For a second or two, maybe three, that seemed like the best idea I'd had all day. When you're going through something like this, you exhibit symptoms similar to someone who has PTSD or someone who has insanity. For that brief moment in time, I couldn't give a nickel's worth of dog meat about that girl's life, the damage I was going to cause my children, and I didn't care about going to jail. Nothing would have satisfied me more than to end her life. But the Holy Spirit said, "Don't do it."

Trust me, ladies, you need the Holy Spirit. During the time of our separation, I would get very lonely, missing my husband, his touch missing and our intimacy. I was given the best sound advice by Gloria when she said, "Be careful not to get into a relationship with somebody else. You are too emotional right now." She elaborated further by saying, "You're used to having a man in your bed. You are used to being around a man and so it would take no time at all before you ended up in bed with somebody."

There were many times in the first two months that we were separated when my husband would come over. My body would ache for him; I was in heat like a dog. He would never show up during the day and wouldn't spend the night. It was, for all intents and purposes, a booty call. He would show up after the kids went to sleep, have sex with me, and make up some reason to leave. It happened several times. I would always cry afterward because I felt like my body would entice him to want to reconcile with me. Your body will not entice your husband into reconciliation. Get that out of your head right now—it is not going to work. The mistress has the same body parts as you. Right now, he's like a kid in a candy store, going to whoever is giving up the free candy. That's where he's going to spend his time or, at least, a few minutes of it. I had to build up enough strength and courage to tell him we could no longer be intimate. It was stunting my growth, giving me false hope, keeping my emotions unstable, and really an ineffective strategy to win him back. You will not win his heart through your body parts; remember, he's already been there, done that.

Sex was probably not the reason he left in the first place. Another reason why I stopped having sex with him was because he was having sex with me and her in the same week. If my goal was to win his heart back, I was defeating my own purpose. I was fighting with the wrong tool. Sex will only meet his physical needs, not his mental and emotional needs. I remember one weekend, we drove to LA together. He came to our home really late at night. I was thinking he had probably been with her; but again, using my body as a means to no end, I totally set him up. I put on the skimpiest shorts that I could find, I knew how attracted he was to my figure. I got exactly what I deserved but not what I wanted—sex and not his heart. On the drive down, we literally did nothing but fight. We were brutal and disrespectful. We were knockdown drag-out nasty about each other. So the effort that I put in to get sex and an emotional connection out of him blew up in my face.

Men don't think of sex the way we do. Especially if they are not in love with the woman they are having it with. When you're separated, he's not invested in working on the marriage or going to counseling. Separate your bodies as well. The more you sleep with him, the harder it will be for you to focus on the things that you need to focus on. Your ability to make decisions will be in utter confusion because you're unable to separate your emotions from the facts. You have to physically disconnect from him as well. You have to be able to hold him accountable. To be able to create boundaries and set expectations. You have to be able to use discernment to determine what your next move will be. As long as you are sleeping with him, you will not make any good sound decisions. And unfortunately, he'll jump at the opportunity to have sex with you out of familiarity. It doesn't mean it's the right thing to do. He'll still get up and leave!

In order to have the best chance at winning back the heart of your husband, you have to do some digging within yourself. Begin to own those areas within your character that he had been challenging you on. That attitude problem, that selfishness issue, the depression, my-way-or-the-highway attitude. It's time to work on those issues that have been an issue for so long, you think they're normal. Those issues that have laid dormant for so many years, you need the help of a therapist to dig them up. Once you begin to work at becoming a better person, you'll realize it's not just for him. He's only a benefactor of the outcome. He was only the push you needed to start doing the work. It's not for you to tell him, "See, look what I've done, honey." Know that once you start truly working on the different character flaws, he'll see them without you having to say a word. The self-improvements will benefit him and everybody around you.

Invest in books about how to pray for your husband, marriage, yourself, and your children. Purchase books on how men think and why they behave the way that they do. I would purchase audiobooks and they helped me to understand my husband and how he thinks, how to communicate with him effectively, and gain a better insight to his emotions. Most importantly, what he needs from me. Up until then, I really didn't know the various sides of men. You have to study your husband in order to best meet his needs. He should be studying you as well. We as women try to make them more complicated than they really are, as complicated as we are but that's not the case. He doesn't react to our emotions and tears. Choose to have those important conversations with him when you are not overly emotional.

I really began to pray for my husband while we were separated. I prayed for him so much, it felt like he was there with me. I know it's hard to speak positive things and to believe better will come when

I CHOSE TO WAIT

things are so out of control and pain but that's what faith is. Speaking things that be, not as though they are. Another thing that I did was begin to make preparation in the home to make room for him before he had even decided to come back. My youngest son, who was probably seven or eight months at the time, slept with me. I moved him into the room with his brothers because I was preparing a place for my husband. Seemed so simple but that was my faith in action. Those types of faith moves will also give you hope.

God sees your actions as well as your intentions. The Bible says God will give you the desires of your heart. In my prayer time with the Lord, I would say, "Lord, having my husband back is the desire of my heart. You did not give me these kids to raise on my own, I expect you to bring him back. We can raise our children together and not in a separated, divorced, or blended family situation." I was very specific and direct in my prayers to God. I didn't play around with what I felt I needed from the Lord. I put it out there, "Lord, bring my husband back. He's the father of our children, I don't want another man raising our sons. I don't want our children split-up. I don't want to have to make arrangements for them to be with their father. I want my husband, the father of our children, to be the only man raising our children."

In your prayers, be specific; write things down that you want to pray about and pray about them continuously. Until you start to see things happen. God hears your prayers and He is on the side of the marriage staying together. He is going to invest in what He created. The Father is always fully invested, even when we are not! *He* is there, working behind the scenes. It is a fight, it is a bloody battle to win your husband back when he is in the arms of another woman. This will cost you what feels like blood, sweat, and buckets of tears. Maintain poise and self-control at all times. Never resort to physical violence. Don't let anyone or anything pull you out of character, if you weren't that hood-rat chick, jumping on cars and fighting in the street when he met you or during the course of your relationship. Don't imitate that behavior because of what you're going through.

I still wonder how I would react if I saw her again. Would I be cool like Sheila in that bathroom scene in *Why Did I Get Married* or straight up ratchet like Tasha? Your reaction can build or destroy. Think about that when the situation is heated. If you become aggressive and uncontrolled, that will only escalate the situation and the result could very well be in a way that you lose out on the ability to reconcile. You never want to present such a disparate behavior. Ultimately it shows your fear and intimidation. She is not the problem, only a symptom of larger complex issues inside the marriage that had been ignored and overlooked for a long time. You probably spent many years arguing and then using make-up sex to put a Band-Aid on it instead of talking through it like adults and even seeking therapy. That bone was fractured, then broken, for years. You just learned to walk with a limp.

The mistress is the outcome of the mismanagement of your marriage. Always take pride in who you are as a woman and how you carry yourself and handle situations. Always guard your heart. Violence may turn in a way that you didn't suspect. The outcome would cost more than you anticipated. All because you didn't take the time to think and assess what may happen. When you resort to being physically violent, you take God out of the position of control and authority and you put yourself there. It's like taking your prayers back. Now this is something *He* needs to work on within you and that could be delaying the process and the outcome that you want. All you did was cause a setback. Take out anger and frustrations in your prayer time. Not face-to-face with your husband or on the phone with him.

For the love of God, please don't talk about your marriage on social media. That is so immature, silly, and childish. If you do that, stop immediately and grow up! Don't seek sympathy from people on social media. Half of them heffas (heifers) probably liked him low-key or made a pass at him anyway. Everybody doesn't need to know your business. Now is the time to grow up. Work on you. Work on the character flaws that the Lord has revealed to you that need to be worked on and worked out. The areas where your husband has mentioned to you that he finds unattractive must be evaluated.

Do not be afraid to go to therapy. An actual licensed therapist, not your mother who's never been married or married multiple times and lives with her boyfriend or your single best friend or coworker. Do your best to find a Christian therapist. Buy a notebook and begin to journal so that you can keep track of things that you prayed about and discussed with your therapist, things that you've seen the Lord work out on your behalf and journal your progress.

Be careful not to get in the habit of comparing your marriage to the marriage of others. People will tell you anything and paint any picture they want. That doesn't mean it's real. You don't know how strong their marriage is, if they are married. Your concern is the state and position of your marriage. The comparison will only cause you to put more pressure on your husband to be someone who he is not instead of allowing him to be himself. You don't want him to feel like he's less of a man by comparing him to your best friend's baby daddy.

So getting back to my journey. By now, I had found out my husband was cheating while I was pregnant with our fourth son. I had given birth and asked to leave our home. I lived with my grandmother for three months while I was on maternity leave, out of state. Maternity leave was over and I had moved back home. I am sure you are wondering how I just moved back in after I was kicked out. Well, I called and told him I was going back. That was it. It was my house too and I wasn't going to let him take that from me too. My husband was still seeing this woman.

For the first few months, I cried regularly. It was a daily thing for me. He went from being my husband to my enemy. I felt like he hated my existence. The way that he spoke to me was horrible and I would often return the fire. But through trial and error during this ride, I had to learn from them quickly. I would take my frustrations out in my prayer time and I would vent to God. I would talk to my aunt who was a woman of God. When I would talk to my husband, I would keep it civil and mainly about the kids. I had to control my emotions because those were triggers for him to end the conversation prematurely. In his eyes, he had no intention of coming back and our marriage was done. He would threaten me with filing for divorce all the time. He would often compare me to her with her being the better woman. I remember having a conversation with him and telling him he chose the wrong woman and his response was, "No, I didn't."

That knock the wind out of my chest. I never expected to hear that from him. But you will hear your husband speak to you in a manner that is totally unlike him, totally inappropriate and hurtful. But you have to remember, Ephesians 6:12, "For we wrestle not against flesh and blood, but against principalities, against powers, against the rulers of the darkness of this world, against." Know that the enemy does not want your marriage to be reconciled because that is a loss for him and win for God! Know that you have the right to fight for your marriage, so be encouraged.

God has been on my case to write this book for years. I've hesitated and made excuses and procrastinated. It took me many years to let go of the pain, memories, and the struggle. It took me years to be able to trust him again. When/if he comes back, you're still in the battle. It's just a different fight, a fight to the finish. Remember, keep your conversations with him light. If there's nothing going on with you, your health, or your kids, then don't weigh the conversation down with how you feel. Nobody wants to keep hearing someone say the same thing to them over and over. By now, he already knows he's failed you, he knows you want him back, and you're angry as hell. Telling him the same thing repeatedly will only cause him not to want to talk to you.

The separation doesn't get easier but it gets more tolerable. You will gain your peace of mind, and you gain control of your life again. The children will be more settled. As long as they understand that their father did not leave them, then they will manage the situation well. I was actually very surprised at how our children reacted to not having their father at home. They've only ever known me and my husband to be together. There had never been a day when Mommy and Daddy weren't living in the same home and raising them together. Until the day that he moved.

My husband would come and get them on the weekends which gave me time to myself. Time to be more comfortable with doing things on my own. Time to read and study. Time to relax and decompress. I started going to the movies by myself and out to eat by myself. I learned that there is nothing wrong with enjoying yourself, with loving yourself. I was able to get refreshed for when my children came back. Even my husband began to see changes in me becoming more independent. The loneliness was still very much alive along with sadness and bouts of depression. I felt those feelings lived with me. But we have to overcome. You can't let depression be your existence. You can't let sadness be the air you breathe. They don't have to be your constant. Let the joy of the Lord be your constant. "The joy of the Lord is your strength" (Nehemiah 8:10).

I didn't always have someone to hang out with. Relatives and friends didn't always have time to listen to every thought in my mind. You won't have people around you, waiting on you, hand and foot, because your partner left you. Develop a relationship with yourself; it will only make you better.

By now, we've been separated several months. He's still in a relationship with this woman. I saw him on the weekends when I was dropping off the kids. There had been times when she was there from the night before. I knew he had slept with her again. Those instances were extremely difficult. He had moved from his coworker's place because of some violence that took place. He was now living in his own apartment in one of the less desirable areas of town. His car had been repossessed. He looked completely stressed out and lost weight. He no longer looked like the man who left my house in January.

Even if you don't get to have play-by-play information on what's going on in his life, you will be able to tell what's going on based on how he looks, where he lives, and how he lives. You'll know if he's genuinely happy or just faking it based on that. As well as how he looks and behaves. You've known him for years by now, just read the signs in front of you. He doesn't want you to know the truth, but if he's lost weight, drinking, and taking drugs, this dude ain't happy—he's a *hot mess*!

My husband didn't even have food in the house when I would drop the kids off. I had to bring food with me to make sure they had meals during their stay at his place. Most of the time, they hadn't taken a bath since I dropped them off Friday night. This was obviously a very trying time for all six of us. He had started back using marijuana and drinking. He became addicted to cigarettes too. No matter how hard he tried to fake like everything was copacetic—yeah right, buddy. You don't even have food to feed your kids.

Those things in itself tell you that you are dealing with someone who has emotional and psychological issues. They are not content with their situation, their decisions, or the pain they have caused. He would stay up late because he couldn't sleep. Wouldn't fall asleep until the wee hours of the morning and would end up late for work because he overslept. It's only by the grace of God that he didn't lose his job through all of this. He had no vehicle, taking the bus to and from work. Through all of this, I was still praying that he would maintain his job as we have four kids to support.

The Winds of Change

Our separation was for a season of eleven months and about twenty-eight days. Things had become bearable. I could now sleep at night without him. I didn't expect to see him when I got home. I knew that I didn't have to call him and talk to him every day, even though I missed him. I still had times where I felt like my heart was literally bleeding because he's not there. I had a routine and kept myself busy, motivated, and functional. I kept in contact with some family members and a few friends.

Love and the right support are very important. You don't realize how much you need family and friends until you really need them. The relationship between me and my mother-in-law has always been strained and dry to the point of choking. I say this because she has never made an attempt to embrace me as her daughter-in-law. I felt like she only saw me as the woman taking her son away from her. Not as a daughter but competition for his attention. I knew that I couldn't rely or depend on her to comfort to me. I knew that no matter what the circumstance was, she was on his side. Even if her son was actively having a sexual affair with a woman outside of me. It's sad but true. I really had no support from his side of the family.

Your Physical and Psychological Health

During your season of separation, keep yourself motivated, encouraged, in shape. Don't conveniently use this time to eat your feelings on a regular basis. If you are seriously overweight, go to the gym. If you have a healthy weight, maintain it. Don't pick up thirty pounds because your husband or wife left. A part of keeping them interested in coming back is your physical appearance. That's what helped attract them to you in the first place. This may keep your partner intrigued to see that you are maintaining your health. You are keeping yourself up and not letting the situation beat you down to a point where all you do is eat and gain weight.

Let's be self-controlled in our eating and disciplined about our appearance. When you see him or her, be presentable. If he comes to pick the kid(s) up on a Friday morning and you're in your pajamas, please bathe and change your clothes before he drops them back off on Sunday. Also don't get in the habit of skipping meals. I know that when something's on our minds, we can get so inundated with our thoughts that we skip meals or have no desire to eat. Keep up your strength; eat regularly like you would if your spouse was there.

CREATE BALANCE IN THE HOME

Spend time with your kids, they still need that love and support. They will need that extra attention now that Daddy is not there. They don't understand what's going on. You don't want them assuming that they had something to do with the separation. Check the temperature of your home to ensure that the children are not showing signs of anxiety or depression. When the children spend time with Dad, the novice may be included. Accept that you can't control who he has around your kids. You can and should have conversations with your spouse to try to ensure that the person or people they have your children around are safe and healthy. Do not avoid those kinds of conversations. I would ask my children if they felt that she was a nice person. If she said anything mean or insensitive to them. Don't interrogate them with going too much into detail. It's not their place to fill you in on what's going on with your spouse or the person that he/she is choosing to be with. I wanted to ensure that my children were not subjected to ignorance or violence. You never know what the other person involved in the affair would do or say to drive a wedge between your spouse and their children.

A lot of times the paramour in the affair has children. It makes you wonder how a person could be so inconsiderate. You think, *How dare you try to interfere with my marriage knowing that your marriage or relationship was dissolved and you had children*? Just remember that an enemy doesn't have common sense or think rationally but out of pure selfishness. People have this mentality of "Well, it didn't work with you but it will work with me." In my situation, the adulteress attempted to study me and study areas or character flaws that my husband divulged to her. She tried her best to be the opposite of who

I was. But that gets tiring and you can't be yourself when you're so busy trying to be unlike somebody else.

I never really knew much about her, except for her name; she had two children. I believe she had been divorced. I remember asking my husband if he was prepared to raise and be financially responsible for six kids, trying to bring common sense in the equation. Did you think about that? Did you spend time considering the fact that if you continue going on with this person, it would be added responsibility? He was already having a tough time being emotionally and financially responsible for our four kids. People that engage in affairs are only after the immediate gratification that they get. Attention and secrecy that they get. It's a very self-fulling relationship. No one's thinking about how it's going to affect or infect our kids. Or how a divorce would impact our lifestyle. It's like they live in a world of their own that is completely void of rational thinking, morals, obligation, or responsibility. Certainly void of God.

Unfortunately the children are dragged along for the ride, impacted emotionally and scarred as well. My middle son was about eight when this was happening. One day, while the kids were visiting their father, the paramour was sitting on my husband's lap. He lived in a very small studio apartment. He had nothing there but a small sofa. For some reason, she thought it was a good idea to be affectionate in the front of our children. My son went to my husband and told him that he didn't like it. I was amazed at the boldness of my son because he knew that relationship was out of order. He knew that this woman shouldn't have been there. Should not have been sitting on their father's lap. I am grateful that my son had a close enough relationship with his father to be able to verbalize how he felt about what he saw. There was another time when I came to pick up the kids and she was there. My husband didn't want me to come in and was being rude and mean. He was blatantly being disrespectful to me to hurt my feelings. I cried all the way to the car and my son heard it and saw me and asked me if I wanted him to go talk to his father. That was amazing. I didn't let him but that was amazing; he wasn't even a teenager and showing such much maturity.

Me

Now I am going to spend some time talking about me. My husband came in while I was writing this and he said, "Are you giving my side of the story? Are you addressing how you behaved before and during?" At first, I was very hesitant because, of course, I want to be seen as the victim and hero of my own story. But in all honesty, he's right!

I grew up being the only child for the first thirteen years of my life. My parents never married and were in their late teens when they became parents. I was living with my grandparents. I always lived with my grandparents; prior to about the age of four, my mother took care of me. My father was "there" but wasn't consistent. My grandfather, who was not my mother's father, molested me from four to nine. He had also raped and molested my mother throughout her childhood, and I am not sure how old she was when it stopped. My mother has passed away and there are many questions that I will never be able to have answers.

I say raped because he was much younger when my mother was being assaulted. I am telling you this because I am trying to give you a background on how and what formed my character. How it was developed and deformed. The memories of what he did to me and how he touched me and introduced me to sexual things and behaviors when I was nothing but four feet tall is disgusting. The fact that it was with him is vehemently vile and vicious.

Fast-forward to my teenage years, I'd never told a soul but my mother that I had been molested. My mom responded by saying, "He molested me too." I later found out the he was a serial pedophile. She was being sexually assaulted by him and his younger brother. She became a drug addict in her mid to late twenties when I was about seven or eight. She stayed on drugs until she died of a massive stroke and brain bleed three weeks after we had buried her younger sister. She never went to therapy, she instead used men, cocaine, and alcohol as coping mechanisms. Because of her addictions, she was never the type of mother who was responsible and supportive of me. Her drug addiction was her life. She stayed in and out of jail. I remember visiting her in jail when I was a child and putting money in her books. Buying her personal hygiene items, shoes, and socks.

I did not have great childhood by any means. I went from one horror story to another. Now we're going to go through high school where I lost my virginity, contracted a sexually transmitted disease, went through severe depression and extreme weight loss. I found out that my boyfriend was cheating on me. I didn't know how to process the pain other than starving myself. By this time, I'd had several boyfriends where the relationships didn't work out for one reason or another. But there was a common theme among them—the phrase "you are controlling." Even my husband tells me that I'm too controlling. To control something is to possess power over it so that it never rises up against you, never catches you off guard or surprises you. Most importantly, it never hurts you.

Being that my father was not consistent, he would lie to me and tell me he was coming to pick me up or spend time with me and didn't show up. He would be absent from my life for one to two years at a time. I never had a healthy relationship with a man. The only other man in the home was a serial pedophile. He was also an alcoholic. By the time I was old enough to date, I had two men who were close male relatives and not healthy, who were emotionally, mentally, and psychologically damaging to my overall well-being. The circumstances were breeding a controlling spirit inside of me. I had been groomed by men not to trust men. I had been groomed by men to control what they had the ability to do in my life. I had been groomed by men that I was not lovable or someone worth taking care of or cherishing. It was also apparent that I would be a controlling woman. The strangest thing to me was, looking back on all this, that I had codependency issues as well.

At the age of nineteen, I met my husband. There I was, young, healthy, and attractive physically—not emotionally as far as intimate relationships go. I had hidden the molestation consciously and subconsciously. I buried it. It was almost like it didn't happen. Not knowing how much of an impact the abuse and the absenteeism of my father would affect/infect my relationships with men. I used my body to get their attention and hoped they would stick around. I didn't know much more about men outside of what they were physically attracted to. Again I had no healthy male role models to teach me what men wanted in a woman, what men liked outside of the physical attraction, how a man should treat a woman inside of an intimate relationship. Outside of knowing how to get a man, I didn't know how to keep them.

It would be many, many years into the relationship with my husband before I would begin retracing the steps of life and putting the puzzle pieces together. One of the pieces of the puzzle read, "I had pushed him away so much that he sought refuge in another woman." I know it seems as though I am taking responsibility for my husband's affair. By no means do I believe that I am responsible for that decision or the decisions that followed. At the end of the day, he made a choice to talk to her, spend time with her, and sleep with her. I wasn't a part of that process. However, I do take responsibility for the fact that even in my early twenties, I did not take advantage of the opportunity to go to counseling. I did not invest in my own psychological health to *help* me figure out why I was the way I was, why I made the decisions I made. Instead I used my grandmother as a role model on how to be a wife, even though she was married to a pedophile. She never hesitated to speak her mind, no matter how verbally abusive she was. She controlled her husband. She had also been sexually assaulted as a young girl and never really spoke to anyone about it, let alone sought a mental health counselor.

As adults, we have to stop taking the common things that people are saying about us so lightly. If you have different people, who do not know each other, use the same word or phrase to describe who you are, then you need to look into that. You need to do some excavating into your past to figure out how you came to be that way.

So getting back to me. I had been raised by a grandmother who had been raped as a child, was an alcoholic, married to a pedophile, with six kids of her own. They were all much older than me but most of them were still in the home. She did stop drinking and smoking when I was young. I never really knew why she handled stress with anger and hostility. Why she cursed like a sailor. Why she was never satisfied or why she never took blame or apologized or was affectionate. But I took on those character flaws. I didn't find out until I confessed to her that I was angry with her for not taking my mother and me out of the household. That she had been raped.

We emulate what we see our parents do, and as young people, we don't realize that they are not the healthiest people to duplicate. Then we repeat those unhealthy patterns and habits as adults in our relationships. The reason I bring all this up is because I'm trying to show you that there are causes and effects for why we think and act the way we do as adults. Why we unconsciously or subconsciously sabotage relationships.

If I had received help early in our marriage, I am positive that our relationship would have been stronger. I would have played my part in the marriage better. That in itself would have allowed me to know that I did everything I could to be a better wife and not just someone who contributed to the damage in our marriage. I would have had the opportunity to talk to someone about how I saw men. How I viewed men in my life. How I needed to have control in a relationship with men because of the neglect and abuse caused by my father grandfather. The combination of hurt between these two men had a devastating impact on my emotional well-being. It was detrimental to my outlook on relationships when it came to men.

Statistically speaking, my life and the things I had going through would render me unable to be a person able to handle marriage. If I couldn't trust a man that I could see, how would I trust God who I could not see? But God has a way of turning ashes into beauty. He knew that in spite of what I had been through, there was still no way that I could live without Him. He had total confidence in Himself and in me. He knew I would not turn from Him. I had been hurt, depleted, and devastated by men. But what did God do for me was give me restoration through my prayer, the Word of God, a restored marriage, and gave me a peace that surpasses all understanding. His Word never returns void (Isaiah 55:11).

Even after all these years, it's not easy for me to talk about the molestation. To remember the things that happened to me and who was behind it. It's not easy for me to dredge up the past. But my goal in this book is to be as open and transparent as I can to help you. I'm sure some of you, better yet many of you, reading this have been molested and/or raped as well. No matter how hard you try, you cannot forget it and you can't self-heal. If you're not seeing a therapist, I urge you to go get help. You also can't self-medicate it away. Leave those prescription pain pills alone. Leave the drugs and alcohol alone. Stop overeating. People are heavily addicted to food, trying to numb the pain. Yes, it's hard to relive; yes, it's hard to talk about; it's hard rehash the details of the sexual abuse.

Reliving the details of the abuse through therapy felt like I was in a war for my life and my sanity. The pain of the memories was that extremely intense. You're testing yourself to see how strong you really are. Can you bear it again? Can you overcome it and heal from it? Can you get delivered from the trauma to be able to help someone else? Because I went through it, I am able to talk about it now. You will come out stronger. I can talk about waking up out of my sleep because he was fondling me at four and five years old. I can talk about him putting his beer-soaked tongue in my mouth and calling me his girlfriend. I can identify with those of you who've gone through the same things.

Hiding it as adults doesn't help. If your spouse or parents, siblings, don't know you were molested, tell them. Even if you're separated, tell them. In the case of your spouse, tell them without expectation. You are only giving them insight as to what happened to you as a child and how it impacted you as an adult. It may give them a better understanding as to why you did or said some things; they may get revelation from it. That can even create a much-needed dialogue between the two of you. It may cause your spouse to open up and reveal secrets in their past they have never shared with you. But don't leave it with them. That is just a step in the right direction. The next step is making an appointment with a counselor and going to your therapy sessions.

Some of us ladies spend $25 to $150 on makeup and clothing. On one pair of shoes or a weave. Now we need to readjust what we invest in. What will give us long-term satisfaction. What will not wither away or be donated to Goodwill in six months. Our emotional and psychological well-being needs repair. Reallocate how you spend your money and invest in yourself. So is the impact of being molested rotting in your mind, contaminating your relationships really worth it? You're not alone. There are many of us who can share in this experience.

As I said before, my mother was raped by my grandfather. She never got help. Her experience, I believe, was horrific. I am certain that what I went through, in comparison to her abuse, was much less traumatic. She wasn't very attentive to me after about the age of nine and quite possibly even before then. I was just too young to know what or how a mother should be. Or what I needed from my mother. I know that she spoiled me and gave me things instead of her. Around the time I turned nine, she was introduced to cocaine by one of my grandmother's friends. And for the next thirty-two years, she was a cocaine addict, alcoholic, in and out of prison until she passed away. The impact of her molestation stole her life from her and those who love her. Prevented her from being a mother, sister, daughter, and a wife. She could not get past that wall of post-traumatic syndrome. She had triggers, and looking back, I think she may have been bipolar. My grandmother was one of her triggers. She would get sober from drugs for maybe two years at a time and something would happen. You never knew when the relapse was coming or why but there was a connection between her being around my grandmother for any length of time and then using again. It was like reliving the same day because of how common my mother's relapses had become. Looking back on stories that I've heard, my grandmother knew her husband was actively molesting her daughter. I think that the history between them and never getting help would continue to be a trigger for my mother.

At this point, there has been generational sexual abuse from my grandmother to me. I got help. One of the most harmful impacts of the molestation on my marriage was being frigid. I was unable or unwilling to be sexually aroused and responsive to my husband. Before marriage, we had no problem. He would even tell me no sometimes. Once we got married, it was like someone performed an operation on that part of the brain in women that causes sexual stimulation or just plain sexual interest and removed it. I had absolutely no interest in sex. You would think that was one of the driving forces behind his decision to cheat but it wasn't. For years, he was loyal to a fault. He says the reason he cheated was because I was controlling, mean, and cold. For years, we would have sex once a month. He tried to convince me of the need for it. How a nonsexual relationship impacted him. He even tried talking to my grandmother about it. Nothing changed. And it wouldn't change for years. I cried out to God, begged Him to, and nothing happened.

The side effect of being sexually abused can appear in many forms in your adult life. But something that happened in your past should not control your present. They are now memories. Memories of events in the past that hurt us. A memory should not control you. You have the right to choose to heal from it. If that person is still alive, you may even consider confronting them. You should confront them. Let them know that you know and remember what they did to you. One thing my therapist challenged me to do was to tell my immediate family members about the molestation. That was one of the hardest things for me to do. But when you do, you take control back, you take power back. Stop protecting everybody but yourself. Expose the secret. As long as it's a secret, you will never heal from it and will never completely move on. You inevitably remain stuck in time.

Getting back to what this book is about. It's been about six or seven months since we separated. This process had allowed me to have a closer relationship with our children. Being a single mother is one of the toughest things a woman can do. To go from my husband being there every day, playing his part with parenting our boys, to literally overnight not having a partner was extremely difficult. The life of a single mother, with managing all the responsibilities of children, school, doctor visits, homework, and day care, that was a full-time job in itself. But every day, you learn something new, you grow and mature. You are able to handle problems better and you gain wisdom from it.

Wisdom is a gift that has been unappreciated. But it's so valuable. Wisdom allows you to not make the same mistakes you made yesterday or last month. When raising children on your own, wisdom is a must. A single mother must know when to ask for help as well as believe that it's okay to stand on your own two feet. Yes, you may not have the money or the ability to go shopping or get your hair done. You learn how to manage money better. You learn how to do your own hair. You learn how to save a few dollars here and there, and at the end of the week, you might be able to go to a thrift store and buy a nice blouse or something that you can dress up. You get those new-to-you items. You learn how to do your own nails. Then when your financial outlook changes, you're not so apt to run out and buy something because you've already become used to managing more on less. Saving becomes the norm. Being a single mother is not a bad thing. It just takes some getting used to, some adjusting, some tears, some loneliness. It is all temporary. It's a trial. Not a permanent way of life.

Now we're heading into fall and I saw him, not as often as I'd like but as he allowed us to. Unfortunately that part of our lives was still under his control. The mistress tried to dominate his free time. So when he had a day off or on weekends, she was sure to make her way to him. That doesn't mean that the Holy Spirit wasn't keeping me on his mind, even though she was in his face. Even though we can't see what God is doing, He is still at work. That was one of the hardest lessons for me to learn. I was still learning that my prayers were still working on my behalf, even though what's going on in front of me may feel like the second level of hell.

October of 2007, I don't remember if I had prayed about it first but I wanted him to come over to the house, spend some time with us, and that had been on my mind and weighing on me for a while. I had no courage to ask him. One day, the Holy Spirit said, "Call him and ask him to come over." I wrestled with it because I felt that my husband didn't want me, he didn't care and wanted to move on. But God gave me the courage to pick up the phone and make the call. I asked him to come and spend the weekend with us. By now, I had learned how talk to him without my emotions. It was almost like talking to a male coworker. I'm not going to overwhelm my coworker with my emotions I'm going to keep it easy and straight to the point. He agreed! I don't even remember him hesitating. I went out and bought food to cook. I bought enough to cook breakfast, lunch, and dinner. He didn't have a car at the time and we lived about thirty minutes apart driving. He had to catch public transportation part of the way and then I picked him up. I rented movies to help keep us entertained and keep the mood in positive perspective. Even though he was there with me, that in itself was a test and a challenge.

Although I wasn't verbally communicating my emotions, that didn't mean they weren't there. They were there and in full force in my mind. It was almost like holding back vomit. You just want to throw up but you know that if you do, you're going to make a mess. Wisdom kicked in and reminded me that if I my emotions came out, it would push him away and he would leave or ruin the opportunity for him to come back in the future. I don't even know how I got through it. I had to keep in mind that the goal was to create an environment where he was comfortable with me and being around me and the kids again. The goal had to come before my emotions. I'm sure he was waiting for me to blow up or start crying or start badgering him about what he was doing. He waiting for an opportunity to prove that his initial decision to leave the marriage was the right thing to do. The goal was saving the marriage and that came before everything else.

Did she call when he was there? Yes. Did she text? Yes. Was it a distraction and a test? Yes. Did my emotions rise up? Absolutely! Were they contained? Unequivocally! I tried not to even mention her. I didn't want the conversations between us to take a negative turn. Not only was it hard not to allow my emotions their due diligence, it was hard not to be intimate with him. It was hard not to touch him like I was naturally accustomed to doing. It was very hard to take him back to the bus stop on Sunday night, knowing she would probably be at his apartment when he got home. Something happened in him when I called him to ask him to come over. Something happened in me that we made it through the weekend without fighting.

The next weekend, he came back. This would be the beginning of our reconciliation and neither one of us was aware. I made sure we had food and entertainment every weekend that he came; he didn't have to ask for anything. He would even bring his dirty clothes and wash them. Sunday night rolled around and I had to drop him off at home or the bus stop. After the first few weekends of him coming over, he would stay until Monday morning. He was more attentive and available to me when he was in the house with me. But when he would go back home, he became distant again. He was struggling between two realms: the realm of being a husband and father versus the second realm of his ulterior lifestyle with his paramour. I remember once telling him that he would be held responsible by God for what he was doing. Deceiving me and this other woman, lying to me and her. For trying to play two sides of the fence and not making a decision and sticking to it. God would hold him accountable for the emotional damage and toll that he took out on both of us. The harm he was causing our children. But I hung in there; I kept in contact with him during the week. I didn't call or text him too much or display that I was upset that he didn't call me back or respond. I had to bite my tongue a lot.

Between October and the end of the year, I don't remember him missing a weekend. Now we're through the holidays and he's still coming over and practically living with us now. We've had our times to talk about what was going on. One thing that I picked up on right away was the fact that he didn't want to own the emotional pain and suffering that he was causing me. He did not want to face the fact that hurt me so profoundly. So at this point, I was tired of him living in two places. I began to push him to make a decision. He would make excuses by telling me he wasn't ready. I dealt with that response the best I could without losing total control of my temper. I have a temper. I knew that I would not tolerate this behavior for much longer. Keep in mind that although I loved him and wanted our marriage to be restored, the separation made me become stronger and okay with not having him in my life as my husband. I had become more independent. I was even making more money than him by this time. I knew that I was young and I could start over again.

It's now December of 2007. I approached him and said, "You need to make a decision, you have to make a choice. I don't want to go into this next year with us not knowing where our marriage stands." The next weekend rolls around and he's due to come back over. I had talked to him earlier in the day. It was a Friday evening and he was supposed to call me so that I could pick him up. He went home and I didn't hear from him for hours. I kept calling and he didn't answer. I sent him a text message and no response. I knew that she was at his apartment. By now, it was nighttime and I was wrestling with whether or not I should go over there.

The enemy will never stop trying even until the last moment. His goal is the destruction of a marriage. Up until the very moment that *victory* came, the enemy was there, fighting me to the end. But Jesus was fighting for me. I got in my car and drove over to his apartment. I was nervous as a deer in headlights. My heart was beating so hard that I could feel it pounding in my chest. I could hear it. I was shaking like a wet cat walking up the stairs to the apartment. I didn't know what to expect. I didn't know if I was about to get into a fistfight with this girl or what. I knocked on the door; he answered, and my husband is much taller than me. He was trying his best to stand in the door at an angle to where I couldn't see who was in there with him. But somehow, I ended up seeing her on his couch. I could see her legs. I said, "What's going on? Why didn't you call me?"

So he went outside and closed the door behind him. He walked me back down the stairs; his apartment was on the second floor. He's trying his best to walk me back to my car. He was trying his best to convince me to go home. He kept saying, "Just go home, just go home and I'll call you."

I said, "No, I need to know what's going on."

By now, we were standing in the driveway in front of my car. His apartment was off the courtyard and you could also see and hear very clearly from where it was. Which meant if she came outside to see what was going on, she would have a clear view. You could also hear two people talking, if they were loud enough, from his apartment. He's still telling me to go home and that he would call me. I was in tears; my heart was broken. Totally confused and hurt all over again. I felt like all my prayers, patience, steadfastness, and endurance had failed. But the promise of God in Galatians 6:9 ("And let us not be weary I n well doing: for in due season we shall reap, if we faint not") was working on my behalf.

Remember I said earlier that even though we can't see what God is doing right then, He is there, still working behind the scenes on our behalf. As I was standing there, listening to my husband try to convince me to go home and ensure me that he would call me, one of the things that stuck out to me was that he also said he was confused about what he was going to do. Me being who I am, I took the opportunity to provide her clarification on his whereabouts over the last three months. Just in case he was getting still digging holes on both sides of the fence. I was about to call his bluff. I said in an extra loud voice, "What about all the time you've been spending with us, coming to my house every weekend, living with us during the week, and all the things you've been telling me? What about all that and how are you confused now?" He did not want me to keep talking. He did not want me to expose the lies he had been telling her. I also have my pride. I wasn't going to stand there all night with any man who wasn't ready to choose me. I don't play second fiddle. I was hesitant but I left. I cried all the way home. I can't remember if I slept at all that night. What kept going through my mind was whether or not he slept with her that night. That was the only thing on my mind.

The next afternoon, I called him at work. I said, "What's going on, what happened to you?"

He said he told her, he didn't know if he wanted to be with either one of us. I was so taken aback. Biting my tongue *again*, I asked him if he wanted to come over; he said yes. I picked him up, he came over, and we talked and talked. I said, "You can't keep doing this, you can't keep playing these games. I'm not playing games with you and you need to make a decision. I don't deserve this and I don't need this."

I believe it was at that moment that he said to me, "I felt like I needed to keep her around, just in case things didn't work out with us."

That was a very honest answer. Immature at best but honest. I reminded him that I wouldn't allow him to keep another woman around. Either he was going to be with me or her. If he was going to be with me, he had to completely eliminate her from his life. When two people have entered into an affair, there is a drawing between them. They are drawn to each other through the soul tie they created—which is not easy to break. He had a connection to her that I would never understand. But soul ties can be broken. He understood where I was coming from and the severity of the situation.

That happened in the beginning of December. Now it's after Christmas, I believe on or about December 30. I remember we were next-door at our neighbor's New Year's Eve celebration. We were standing in the backyard, underneath the stars. I asked him again, "What are you going to do?"

He said, "I'm coming home!"

"But they that wait upon the Lord shall renew their strength; they shall mount up with wings as eagles; they shall run, and not be weary; and they shall walk, and not faint" (Isaiah 40:31).

My many, many prayers had been answered! After a few days of him being completely home, I started putting pressure on him to call her and end it. I had him do that in front of me. I don't believe she answered the phone. But I stayed on him to make sure that he verbally communicated to her that the relationship was over. Our next step was getting a new phone number. After that, I was working on ending the lease on the apartment that he had. It felt like a straight miracle from God to go pack up that apartment and bring him home. Although it's been twelve, almost thirteen, years since the affair, the memory of it still makes me cry. And if you're thinking that we lived happily ever after, not quite!

The Return Home

I felt some sense of relief, knowing that my husband had finally come home. However, the emotional toll of the last eleven months was still looming. Yes, he wasn't living in a separate home; I got to see him every day. We slept in the same bed and was able to be together again as husband and wife. But his state of mind was still separate for me. My husband was never 100 percent remorseful for what he had done. He would apologize but it wasn't what I wanted. I think the difference in what I expected and what he was doing was still creating conflict. It took him years to really own it. The sad part about that is, we could have recovered a lot quicker. We could have rebounded in a healthier manner had he allowed himself to be humble and transparent. There was such a hardness about him. That hardness was a hindrance for me to get close to him again. Maybe he felt he wasn't the only one to blame for the destruction of the marriage. Maybe he wasn't ready to let his guard down with the woman he had learned to live without. Maybe I had unrealistic expectations and wanted too much too quickly. When he left, he was very clean-cut, didn't smoke, wasn't a heavy drinker, hadn't smoked marijuana in many years. During our time apart, became a chain-smoker, drank, and lost a lot of weight. He just didn't look like the man I fell in love with. I had an immediate issue with all of that. Those were just the surface issues, the little foxes.

While he was gone, I fantasized about being intimate with him again. Remembering how it felt when we made love. Knowing that my husband knew my body. He knew how to make my body work. He had studied me sexually and knew what would draw me in. But now, knowing that he had slept with another woman, how would I process that when the opportunity came for us to be intimate again?

How would I not turn him down because I couldn't get the images of him having sex with her out of my head? For the longest time, I would cry while we were being extra friendly. There was nothing he could do or say to stop me from crying. Even though he was there with me, we were reconciled, I was still absolutely devastated by the fact that my husband had shared his body with someone else. He wasn't experienced when we met. I was the only woman who knew what he looked like naked. Now someone else new got to experience him. Someone else got to share in the pleasures of what it's like to be with my husband. No person, no therapist, no one can fix that.

It would take a long time for me not to conjure up those images while we were intimate. It would take a while for me to stop crying in the midst of us having sex. I had to fight the feeling that I had the right to reject him. If I did, I could push him away again. That was one of the most difficult things to go through during our process of getting reestablished with each other. That battle was real. It was almost a daily battle. For a while, I had would pound at him day after day, reminding him of the fact that he slept with her, took her places, spent time with her, and how he rejected me. I had every right to speak to him about what I was feeling. For many months, I couldn't say a word about it; but now I had the opportunity, I had the floor, I had the mic—it was my time! What I didn't take the time to realize was that no one wants to hear how they failed repeatedly for months. I was so busy trying to beat him down emotionally that I ended up pushing him away again.

It was about six months after he had come home. He decided he was going to get his own place. He was no longer sure that he had made the right decision to come back. He felt he needed more time to think about whether or not he wanted to spend the rest of his life with me. It totally knocked the wind out of me. We had just come back together and he was already backing out! Of course, I wondered if he had been in contact with her. If she was trying to get him back. It was happening all over again. The feeling of loss, not having any control, not being a part of the decision. He gave me no choice in the matter. After he told me that he was leaving, he followed through. He found another apartment close to his job, thirty minutes away from us. Our finances were divided. I was behind in our mortgage payments, trying to provide for four kids. I was totally blindsided. I thought that he meant what he said.

But everybody's words and promises have a B clause. They have an expiration date. Just because a man comes home doesn't mean he's happy. The other person involved in the relationship always has access to what that B clause entails and can decide to act on it at any given time, if the circumstances do not suit them. With him, I felt like his read, "I know I hurt you, I know you're still upset. However, I will only give you so long to get over it. After that time has passed, if you have not gotten over it, that's your problem not mine. Your issues with what I did are starting to make me upset. I don't want to keep hearing about it, I don't want to go to counseling, you need to figure it out."

My husband did not have a relationship with God which, I believe, is part of the reason why he wasn't as remorseful about his own behavior. Why he wasn't moved to repentance via his own conviction. Or by the Holy Spirit's prompting to make right his wrong. As I said before, he was hardened. His heart was hardened toward me, toward God, and anything that would make him feel. His relationship with his own father has always been strained. Unfortunately his father didn't take the time to teach him how to be a man, teach him how to love and care for a woman. In many instances, his father taught him the total opposite of how to love and care for a woman. How to be sensitive, available, and how to keep his feelings, desires, and passions at home. A lot of what I was seeing from him was a learned behavior.

Everybody knows what is right and what is wrong. But many of us duplicate the lifestyles of our parents, lifestyles of our elders or siblings. I have young relatives today that are alcoholics and drug addicts, even though they saw how those outlets destroyed our grandparents, parents, uncles, and aunts, etc. I'm not giving him an excuse for what he did. I am painting a picture to show you that not every choice we make was made at the time that we made it. Some choices that we make are/were preprogrammed into us to be made at the time where it could destroy us.

My husband and I have a lot of emotional baggage when it comes to relationships. I hoped and prayed that he would treat me as well as he treated his mother. I had always admired their relationship until the day I saw him lie to her. At that moment, I knew that if he could lie to his mother, he would lie to me. He was somewhat of a habitual liar for most of our relationship. He would lie about things he didn't even have to. He would lie so well that it would be a manipulation tactic. I learned early on in our relationship that I couldn't always trust him. I couldn't always take his word for it. Looking back over the course of our relationship, we should not still be together. I'm sure we both could have found others who would have given us less problems and stress than we were giving each other. But, who was to guarantee that?

By no means am I an angel. I was mean and evil as hell. My ego was seven feet high and I'm only five feet tall. I am a total spoiled brat. Too complicated for words to explain. In many aspects, this man should receive a trophy for dealing with me as long as he has. How many of us try to create that perfect person through marriage and end up married three, four times by the age of forty and was not ever a widow? That's embarrassing, silly, and childish. Who is the common denominator in that scenario? I never wanted to have to start all over again with someone else. I/we have dealt with more than the average person would.

It just goes to show you that God can give us grace for anybody. I didn't want to realize; I was still dealing with an immature young man with grown-man responsibilities and expectations. I was too immature to realize that I was with someone who was never taught what it meant to be a husband. We were both going through this marriage thing blindly like most of us are. Neither of us had good examples of what a marriage looked like or how to maintain it. What to expect and how to handle the many issues that will arise over the course of a marriage. I give him total props for choosing daily to stay married. What he wasn't, when we got married and when we reconciled, he is now. He is a man after my heart; he is a man who is sensitive. He is a man who comes home to me every day without fail. He is a man who tells me about his day, he is a man who tells me how he feels, he is happy, he is a man who works through his feelings and his issues with me. He is trustworthy and completely open with me. He is a *man*! I once heard a famous preacher say, "Don't let somebody else take and reap from your investment!"

Going back to him moving out again. He moved out but only spent about a week in that apartment. It wasn't five days straight. It was here and there. Other than that, he was still coming home every day. It ended up being another wake-up call for me. I needed to calm down and back off a little bit. Give him some space to breathe. Give him the opportunity to settle back into the routine and rhythm of married life. The mistress didn't nag him about everything that he did. Even if he hurt her, she still was keeping him first and not her feelings. The lease on the apartment was for six months. It was difficult having to budget, paying for an apartment that he wasn't living in. But what was more important—where he lived or how much we were spending?

Eventually we were able to break the lease without damaging our credit even more. The reconciliation was finally complete. The restoration of our marriage would be a long process and would take many years. We have never gone to marriage counseling. I'm not proud of that. I know that we would have benefited from going to therapy and working out those deeper issues that caused us to lose control and become so out of touch with each other. I believe the only reason why we have survived is because of God. I spent the entire time we were separated on my knees. I prayed for my husband every single day. I also prayed for him throughout the day. I kept him before the Lord. I still pray for my husband. God has to be a major part of your marriage. If you don't know how to pray, you can always buy books or even use Google to look up prayers. Pinterest is a good tool to use as well.

In all honesty, there is no formal way you need to pray to your Lord and Savior. How can you formally pray to the Lord who just heard you curse somebody out? How can you formally pray to God who knows your dirty little secrets? How can you formally pray to the Father who just heard you lie? Can you formally pray to the Father who saw you flirt and/or cheat on your spouse? If you really think about it, you are not formal so how can you pray a formal prayer to the Lord who sees and knows everything. Who knows your thoughts? When you pray, do it with total admiration and respect. Address Him as the highest being in the world because that's who He is. Always be you, be humble.

Humility and love are key in prayer. He already knows what you're going to say before you say it. He already knows your intentions. And He also knows the last thing He told you to do, the last thing He told you to fix, and you still haven't fixed it and you still haven't done it. Be honest with yourself and with God. You cannot manipulate him and you cannot coerce Him into doing what you want Him to do. If you're praying for your husband, He hears what you say about your husband but He also knows what needs to change within you. He knows what it will take for the marriage to be reconciled. He knows what issues need to be corrected in both parties involved in the relationship, not just the person having the affair.

I will share a testimony that confirms God hears your prayers and wants you to allow Him control over your life. He cares about the smallest details affecting your life. Earlier in the book, I mentioned this famous female pastor that I was following while we were separated. She cowrote this book that was written years before I purchased a copy. I didn't know that it would include a CD of her last conference as a bonus with buying the book. I was so excited to hear what was on it. The CD player in my car hadn't been working for several months. I thought to myself, *Let me see if it'll work*. That CD played like the CD player was never broken. As she began to preach about what it meant to be a wife and not a knife, she was so on point with who I was and how my ways were contaminating my relationship. It was so dead-on that I could not listen to the CD all the way through. When somebody is on your street, got your address, phone number, security number, all your passwords, and was never invited over, they had the audacity to record this CD five years before I heard, it was nothing but the power of God.

Just like this book. Some of you may not read it until 2025. My testimony and the things that I have said in this book will be so on point with what's going on in your life. You may not be able to read it all the way through the first time. Your flesh doesn't want to hear the truth about who you are. You definitely don't want to change. But you want the other person to change and adapt. God doesn't work like that. It took me months before I could listen to that CD all the way through without breaking down in tears. This woman knew my business like she had been eavesdropping on my phone calls, like my home had been tapped.

My goal in writing this book was first to honor what the Lord had told me to do which was get it done. He said, "Enough is enough. I've given you plenty of time." Secondly, in hopes that I could help heal marriages, specifically for people who had gone through what I had been through. I personally would never want another woman experience the pain, agony, and betrayal that I had.

Before I end this chapter of my life, I wanted to share one last thing that I remembered while thinking of information, advice, and experiences to add to this book. I lived with my sexual abuser until I was eighteen years old. He died a few months after I graduated from high school. During the final years of his life, his diabetes began to eat away at his limbs to the point that he was completely immobile. I had to bring him food, change his diaper, and look after him. I don't remember once thinking, *I could end his life*. Remember earlier in the book, I said I had buried the abuse so deep it was like it didn't happen. Looking back on that time in my life, I believe God used that so that I would help him when he needed it. I wouldn't be filled with hate and retribution. Even though I could have refused to care for him, based on what he had done, I chose to help. I was more robotic than human at that point but I was still there. Over the course of his final months, he lived in a rest home. He spent his days screaming at the top of his lungs for my grandmother and for God to take him. Every day, he would wail out those things. He was tormented; he had no peace. I didn't cause that, he did.

How many of us do or have done vile and evil things in the eyes of the Lord? Yet He still chooses to love, care for, and forgive us. No one is innocent and without sin. Forgiveness is always the answer. If you do not have a relationship with God and you have not accepted Jesus Christ as Lord, get your Bible out and go to Romans 10:9–

10, "If thou shalt confess with thy mouth the Lord Jesus, and shalt believe in thine heart that God has raised him from the dead, thou shalt be saved. For with the heart man believeth unto righteousness; and with the mouth confession is made unto salvation."

Confess that Jesus is Lord and believe in your heart that God raised Him from the dead. Jesus is absolutely my Lord and Savior, hero, best friend, mother and father, therapist, and my jailer when need be. He is the lover of my soul. He loves to hear from me, He loves to see me, He loves when I wake up in the morning. He just plain loves me. He loves you too.

My Prayer for You, the Reader

Dear Father God, I pray that you would please bless every reader and their marriage that has been affected or infected by adultery. I know that your Word says, the spouse affected by the affair has the right to leave the marriage because of abandonment. But I also know that you are a God of second chances and that there is nothing too hard for you. Father, my ask is that you would please intercede and intervene in those marriages where an affair is actively taking place. Give the grieving spouse the endurance to wait to be reconciled. Give the affected spouse the community and love that they need in order to wait. Surround them with people that will be encouraging and would lift them up in their times of hardship. Remove all the naysayers and those filled with negativity and bitterness from their lives.

Bless them, Father, with peace that surpasses all understanding. Peace when they come in and when they go out. Peace throughout their day and peace while they sleep. Peace is so vital during this time when the enemy is crafty and busy filling their minds with images and thoughts. Remind them to watch what they speak during this vital and sensitive time as words can have a profound impact on the outcome of the situation. I pray that they would go to you during this time and not rely on people who don't have the power to restore their marriages. I pray that the pain would push them to totally trust in you. This time of suffering would be a bridge for them into a lifelong relationship with you. I pray that they will know you are there and you are the only answer in this trail. This test is only for a season. We have no control over how long the season is but we do have control over the growth we achieve during the season. Remind them that you are not in the business of wasting pain. The lesson will be learned. In Jesus name. Amen.

About the Author

Joi Vaughn is a strong woman and child of God. She and her husband have been married for twenty years and they have four children together. They are still striving toward having a great and successful marriage. She believes that the Lord will work all things together for the good of those that love God and are called according to His purpose. Which is why she was able to overcome and conquer the obstacles that came her way during the separation of her marriage. It wasn't easy to see her hurting or hear her crying. But with each passing day, it was a relief and a joy to see her grow stronger. Pain was a tool that God used to teach her some very hard lessons. Pain was a tool that God used to allow her to see her own mistakes. Pain was a tool that God used to show her right from wrong, just like training up a child.

The separation from her husband was an opportunity that God used to finally get her attention that He wouldn't have had otherwise because she wasn't listening. Let's learn the lesson the first time He speaks, at the first prompting and the first reminder, not when all the alarms are going off and the building is on fire or when we hear bombs dropping. We can avoid so many errors, issues, and trials if we would just *listen* when He speaks the first time.

CPSIA information can be obtained
at www.ICGtesting.com
Printed in the USA
BVHW031539180421
605029BV00012BA/950